MUSH!

Mush!

ACROSS ALASKA IN THE
WORLD'S LONGEST SLED-DOG RACE

by Patricia Seibert
Illustrated by Jan Davey Ellis

THE MILLBROOK PRESS · BROOKFIELD, CONNECTICUT

This is the true story of an unusual race. The race is held every year in the big, beautiful state of Alaska. There, all through the long winters, snow blankets the land, and thick ice covers the sea.

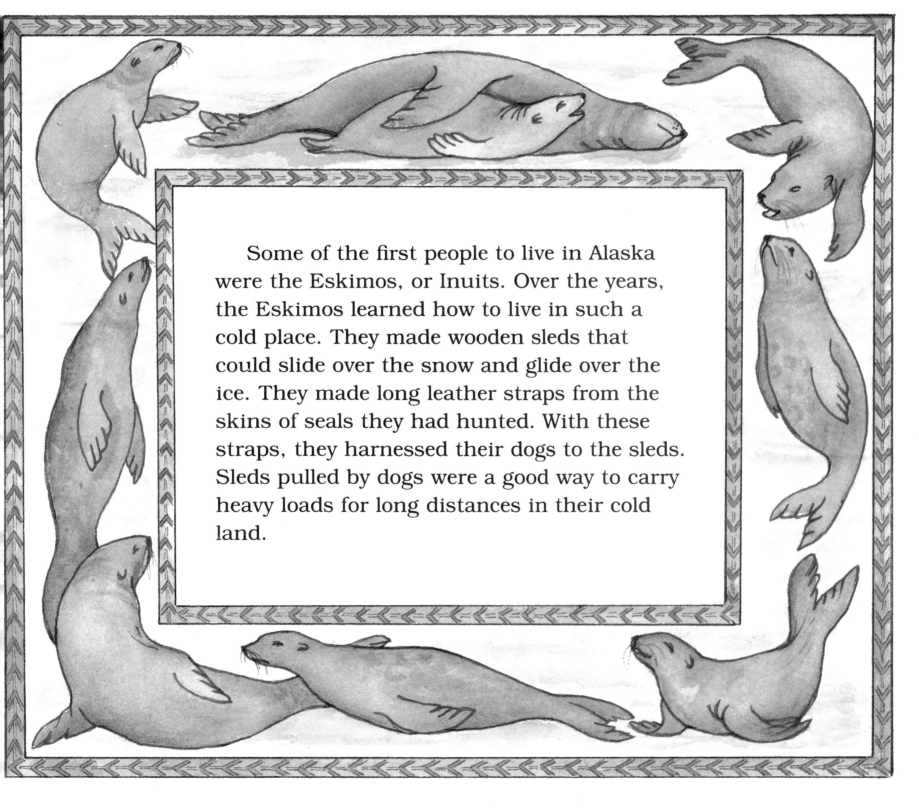

Some of the first people to live in Alaska were the Eskimos, or Inuits. Over the years, the Eskimos learned how to live in such a cold place. They made wooden sleds that could slide over the snow and glide over the ice. They made long leather straps from the skins of seals they had hunted. With these straps, they harnessed their dogs to the sleds. Sleds pulled by dogs were a good way to carry heavy loads for long distances in their cold land.

No one knows where the first Eskimo dogs came from. They looked very much like the wolves that live in the far north. Sometimes a wolf and a dog would have puppies together. Some of the puppies became good sled dogs.

The Eskimo dogs had two coats of fur to keep them warm and dry: an inner coat of short, soft, thick fur, and an outer coat of long, shaggy fur. Their fluffy tails curved up over their backs so that they did not drag in the snow. Their strong legs could carry them over miles of icy ground.

The Eskimo dogs were strong and brave. But even the best sled dogs were not pets. Eskimos kept dogs for the work they could do.

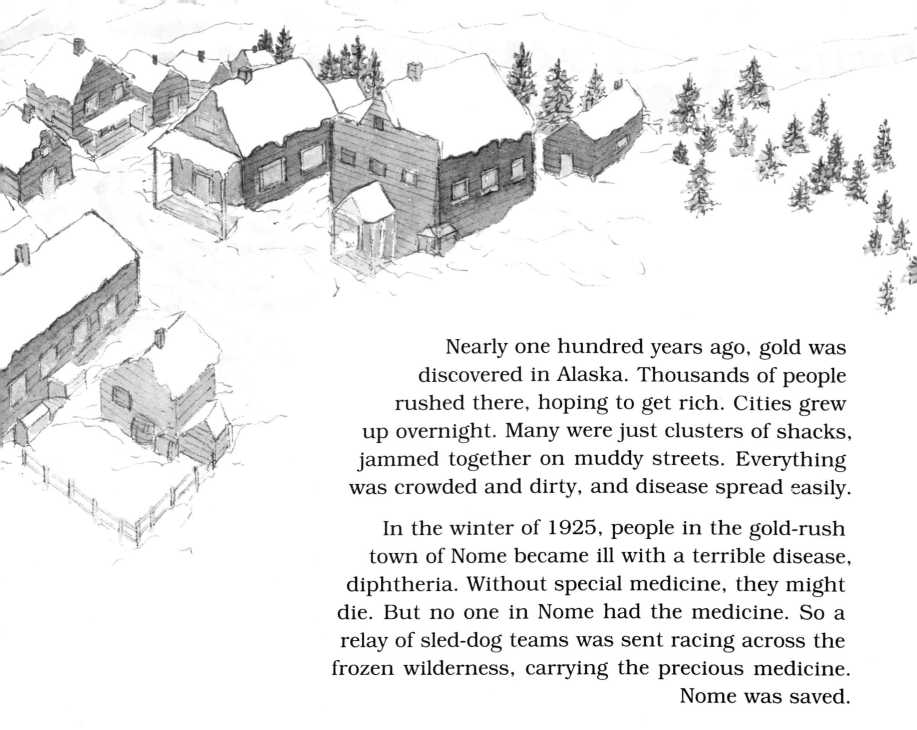

Nearly one hundred years ago, gold was discovered in Alaska. Thousands of people rushed there, hoping to get rich. Cities grew up overnight. Many were just clusters of shacks, jammed together on muddy streets. Everything was crowded and dirty, and disease spread easily.

In the winter of 1925, people in the gold-rush town of Nome became ill with a terrible disease, diphtheria. Without special medicine, they might die. But no one in Nome had the medicine. So a relay of sled-dog teams was sent racing across the frozen wilderness, carrying the precious medicine. Nome was saved.

Years passed. Many things changed in Alaska. The dirty, crowded gold-rush towns were cleaned up, or they faded away. People came to Alaska looking for oil instead of gold. And snowmobiles became a popular way to travel over snow and ice. Few people wanted to train or care for sled dogs.

But one man, Joe Redington, wanted people to remember how important the sled dogs had been. He decided to organize a race to honor the brave dogs that had taken life-saving medicine to Nome. The race would follow an old supply trail, the Iditarod Trail. And so it was named the Iditarod Trail Sled Dog Race.

The first Iditarod was held in 1973. Every year since then, in March, drivers have set out from Anchorage and raced their dog teams across Alaska to Nome. Often more than fifty teams compete. Each is made up of seven to eighteen dogs.

The Iditarod is the longest sled-dog race in the world—more than one thousand miles long. The fastest teams can reach the finish line in eleven or twelve days. Other teams take more than a month. But the trail is so long, and goes through such wild country, that even just to finish the race is to do well.

Drivers work for months to get ready for the race. They spend hours each day training their dogs. In summer, when there is no snow, the dogs pull wheeled carts or all-terrain vehicles instead of sleds. Training often begins when the dogs are just puppies. Older, trained dogs help the drivers teach the young dogs how to pull as a team.

A dog that is especially smart leads the team. This dog must respond to the driver's commands. "Gee" means "turn right," and "haw" means "turn left." The command to start may be "hike!" or "let's go!" In the old days, it was "mush!" For this reason, the drivers are called mushers.

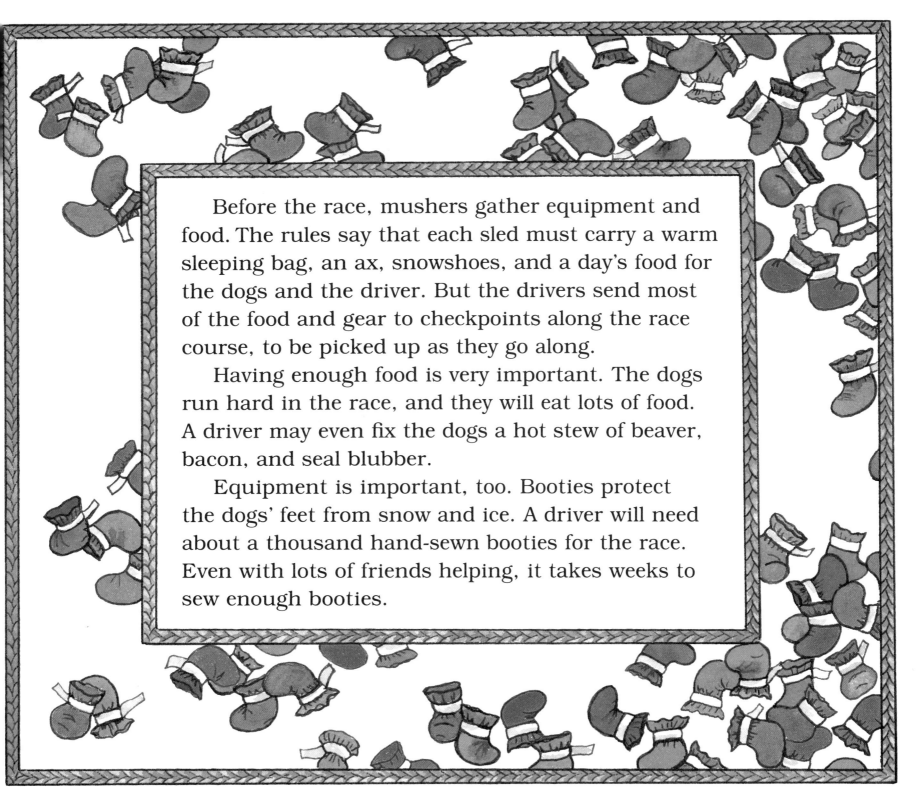

Before the race, mushers gather equipment and food. The rules say that each sled must carry a warm sleeping bag, an ax, snowshoes, and a day's food for the dogs and the driver. But the drivers send most of the food and gear to checkpoints along the race course, to be picked up as they go along.

Having enough food is very important. The dogs run hard in the race, and they will eat lots of food. A driver may even fix the dogs a hot stew of beaver, bacon, and seal blubber.

Equipment is important, too. Booties protect the dogs' feet from snow and ice. A driver will need about a thousand hand-sewn booties for the race. Even with lots of friends helping, it takes weeks to sew enough booties.

At last everything is ready. It's time for the race. Mushers and their teams start out. What lies ahead? Will a moose charge out of the woods into a dog team? Will the ice on a frozen creek give way, dropping musher and dogs into the icy water? Will a sled break?

Will a dog be injured? If that happens, the driver will carry the dog on the sled to a checkpoint where a veterinarian is standing by to help.

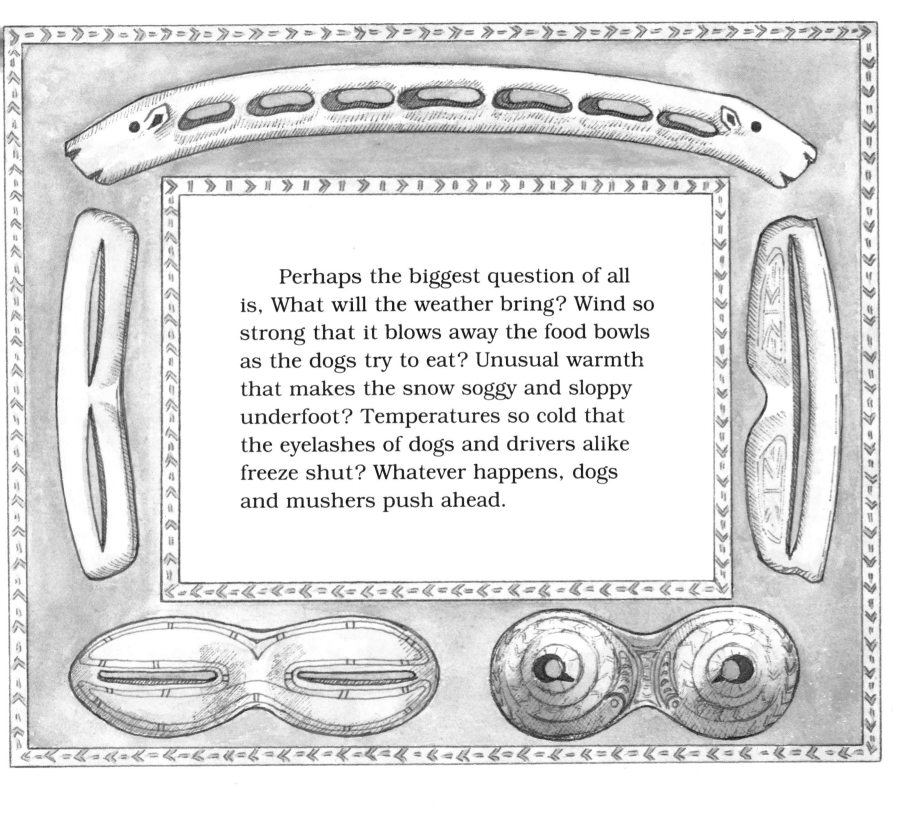

Perhaps the biggest question of all is, What will the weather bring? Wind so strong that it blows away the food bowls as the dogs try to eat? Unusual warmth that makes the snow soggy and sloppy underfoot? Temperatures so cold that the eyelashes of dogs and drivers alike freeze shut? Whatever happens, dogs and mushers push ahead.

ALASKA

EVEN YEAR ROUTE
ODD YEAR ROUTE

NOME

IDITAROD

ANCHORAGE

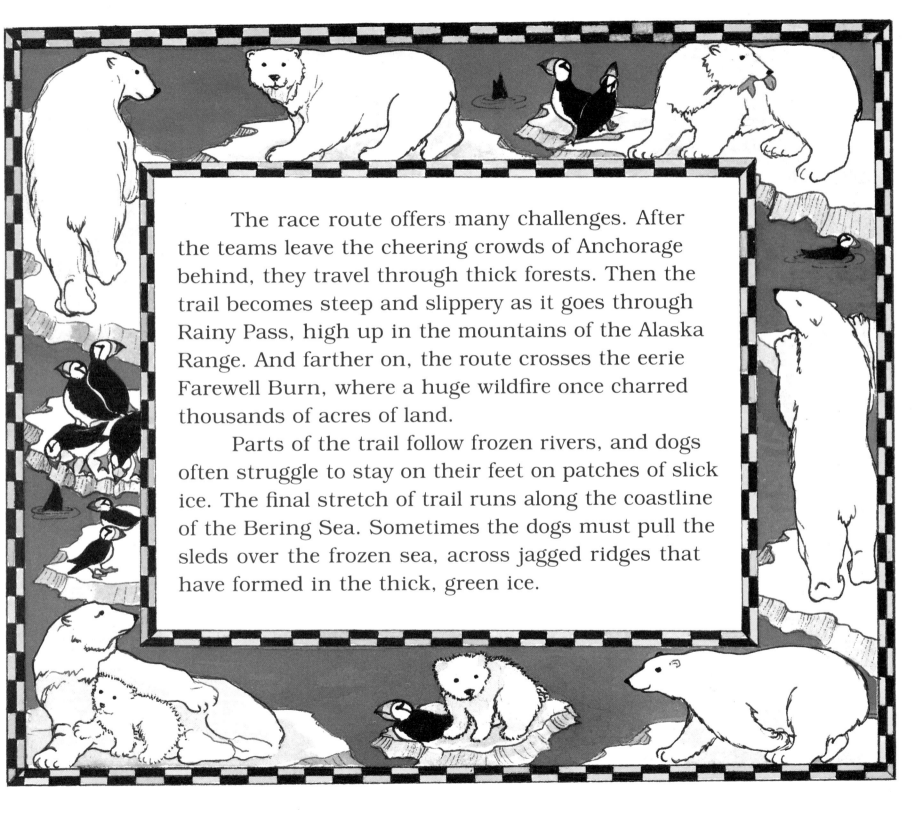

The race route offers many challenges. After the teams leave the cheering crowds of Anchorage behind, they travel through thick forests. Then the trail becomes steep and slippery as it goes through Rainy Pass, high up in the mountains of the Alaska Range. And farther on, the route crosses the eerie Farewell Burn, where a huge wildfire once charred thousands of acres of land.

Parts of the trail follow frozen rivers, and dogs often struggle to stay on their feet on patches of slick ice. The final stretch of trail runs along the coastline of the Bering Sea. Sometimes the dogs must pull the sleds over the frozen sea, across jagged ridges that have formed in the thick, green ice.

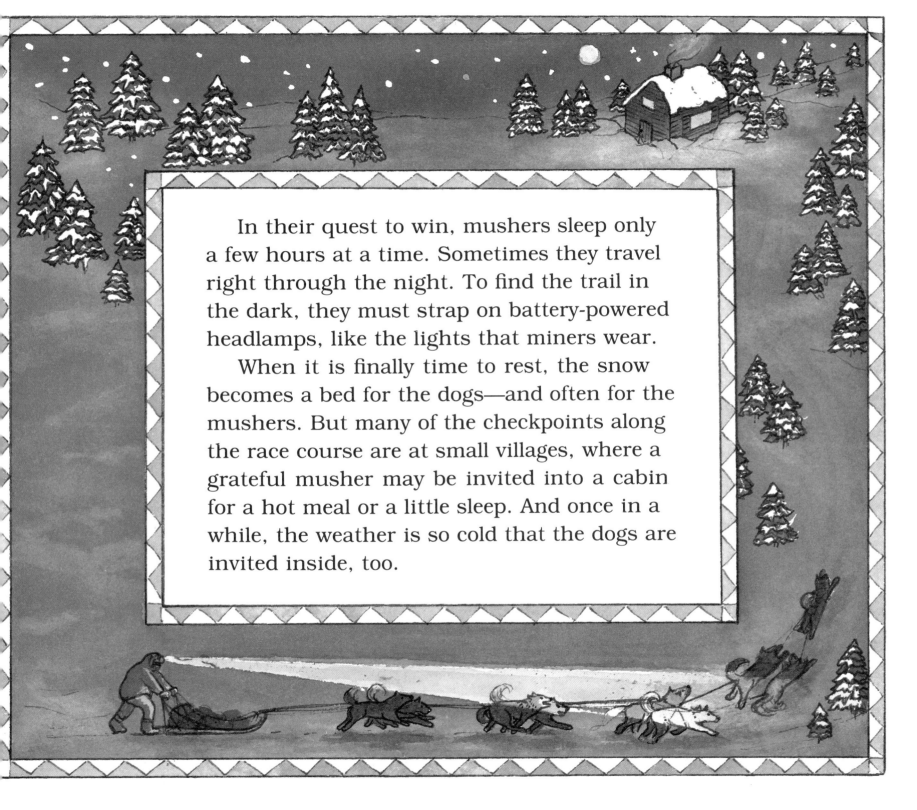

In their quest to win, mushers sleep only a few hours at a time. Sometimes they travel right through the night. To find the trail in the dark, they must strap on battery-powered headlamps, like the lights that miners wear.

When it is finally time to rest, the snow becomes a bed for the dogs—and often for the mushers. But many of the checkpoints along the race course are at small villages, where a grateful musher may be invited into a cabin for a hot meal or a little sleep. And once in a while, the weather is so cold that the dogs are invited inside, too.

Day after day, the mushers drive their dog teams across the wild, frozen land. Each wants to reach Nome first. But sometimes the drivers must help one another.

If fierce winds blow and snow fills the air, the drivers cannot see the trail. Then the mushers take turns in the lead, making a path for the others. As soon as the weather clears, they race against each other again.

At last, after days of racing, the mushers in the lead can see the city of Nome ahead. The race is almost over!

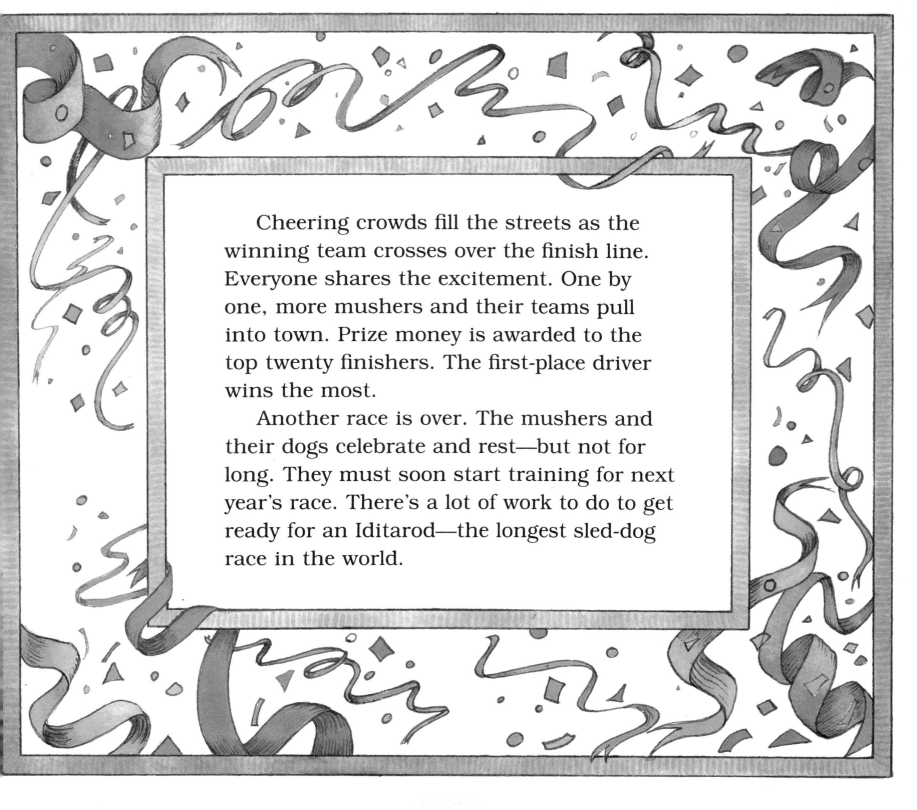

Cheering crowds fill the streets as the winning team crosses over the finish line. Everyone shares the excitement. One by one, more mushers and their teams pull into town. Prize money is awarded to the top twenty finishers. The first-place driver wins the most.

Another race is over. The mushers and their dogs celebrate and rest—but not for long. They must soon start training for next year's race. There's a lot of work to do to get ready for an Iditarod—the longest sled-dog race in the world.

Library of Congress Cataloging-in-Publication Data

Seibert, Patricia.
Mush: Across Alaska in the world's longest sled-dog race/
by Patricia Seibert: illustrated by Jan Davey Ellis.
p.   cm.
Summary: describes the annual Iditarod dog sled race in
Alaska and the sled dogs who compete in it.
ISBN 1-56294-053-8 (LIB.)   ISBN 1-56294-705-2 (PBK.)
1. Iditarod Trail Sled Dog Race, Alaska—Juvenile literature.
[1. Iditarod Trail Sled Dog Race, Alaska.   2. Sled dog racing.
3. Sled dogs.]   Ellis, Jan Davey, ill.   II. Title.
SF440.15.S45   1992
798'.8—dc20   91-38883   CIP   AC